T0145196

Memoirs of A Cat Named

Mr. Riley T. Kitty

BOB A. JACKSON

To order additional copies of this book, contact:
Xlibris
844-714-8691
www.Xlibris.com
Orders@Xlibris.com

ISBN: Softcover   978-1-6698-0841-1
        EBook   978-1-6698-0840-4

Print information available on the last page

Rev. date: 02/24/2022

Memoirs of A Cat Named
Mr. Riley T. Kitty

Introduction

This is a story about the relationship of a man and a cat. The man was more of a dog person than a cat person in the beginning of their relationship. Over time, the cat started showing more affection and trust for the man. Eventually, their relationship grew into a total friendship between the two. Over time the man often wondered what the cat was thinking when it sat and just stared. That man is me, Bob A. Jackson, and the cat is Riley sometimes called "Mr. Kitty" by other members of the family. The following story is one of education, understanding, and love. It is entirely one man's opinion of what it could be if a cat could talk.

As you read the story, there are a few notes that need to be explained. First, anytime that the writing is in regular font, those are the author's words and thoughts. When the font is in bold, those are the words and thoughts of the cat. In trying to express what a cat might think or say, the words used will be the same as a human would say. That's the only way this entire writing would make any sense. Much of the information shared/written is the author's opinion. Most of the educational writing has been from google on the internet or personal interviews. It's information that is out there for anyone to use. Many hours were spent researching and evaluating sources before they were actually used to complete the writing.

One of my goals in writing this story is an attempt to show the readers a new perspective and appreciation for cats. They are a very unique living animal made for unique purposes in our lives. The intent is to explain what they might think and feel while living in our world. I hope that you will find it entertaining, educational, and humorous at times. This writing is intended for all ages...young to old. I still love dogs, but through this writing experience and living with Mr. Riley Kitty for twelve years, I have learned a whole new appreciation and admiration for cats.

I recently discovered a cross like figure on Riley's back. The cross figure is black with white hair all around it. It's not a perfect cross, but once it is pointed out to someone, they can see it very easily. It's amazing to me that we've had Riley for over ten years and are just now discovering this on him.

Enjoy the ride and let's get started.

Bob A. Jackson

DISCLAIMER: The entire idea and thoughts/opinions for taking this approach to writing about cats came strictly from the author. To my knowledge, no cats were killed or injured due to the writing of this work, nor is the same statement to apply after it's published and read by others. However, from my experience in writing this book, if a cat could read it, I'm pretty sure their sensitive feelings might be hurt on some of the comments and cat responses that I made. If they could read, my wish would be that what I said about them for the most part would be acceptable in their complicated minds.

Bob A. Jackson

January 10, 2022

Hello! My name is Riley. I've also been called Mr. Kitty by my human family. I was named after a television character on a show called "The Life of Riley" back when there were only black and white televisions in the late 1950's. I am a male black, white, and golden brownish tan Tabby. I've been here on earth for about twelve years. I weigh in at about 14 pounds. I have a long tail with perfectly spaced rounded circles the full length. My owner just recently discovered a large size cross on my back. There is dark hair in the shape of a cross that is outlined with all white hair. He said that he could not figure out why he had missed it before now, but maybe it was that it really was too large to discover it. All four of my paws are white. Guess I could have also been named "Socks", but that would have been too ordinary for a special cat like me. My eyes are greenish gold. I have a small brown spot on the left side of my nose. Have no idea where that came from. There is a small scar that starts right below my right eye and goes halfway across my nose. I'll tell you more about how I got that in the story. I'm told that cats have nine lives and I'm sure that I've used up a few of those over the years. I hope you enjoy reading my story and laugh many times while reading it.

Riley

Riley Memoirs-Book Description

This book could be described as a non-fiction, true experience with a twist on learning how to take animal-human behavior to the next level.

The author has taken a different approach in writing this book about cats. Meet Riley and learn about his world as seen through the eyes of the author. This idea came about one day as Riley was looking up to the corner of the room ceiling. He became mesmerized and intently focused staring at whatever he saw there. That look in his eyes caused an immediate thought from the author's perspective. "What in the world could he be seeing or imagining at that very moment?" This question kept repeating itself to a point that the author started watching more closely the cat's behavior and reactions to various events in the cat's daily life. After making these observations, the author started experiencing a closer bonding relationship with the cat. After a while longer that experience led to the writing of this book. One other unique feature of the book is the explicit detail in which the author explains how to totally please and pleasure a cat. People, old and young, will learn step by step how to win a cat's unique personality over to their side of the thinking game. Hint: the reader will learn to appreciate the importance of patience and very gentile touches with loving actions. Those are two very specific behaviors that every human being would benefit from for making some amazing changes in their own life.

Table of Contents

(Note: Substituted for chapter numbers are subtitles related to that writing.)

Do Cats Really Have Nine Lives?

This is a question that some people have a problem in understanding what it really means. Originally, this concept may have been conceived in Egypt where cats became worship idols over time. At about the same time, cats appeared in China. At one time in early Egyptian history, cat idols were proclaimed to be evil animals and brought bad luck to those who owned them. This led to almost a complete annihilation of the animal in Egypt. In China, cats became revered over time and were given the number nine on the zodiac calendar used in their culture. Number nine means "lucky". This number was more than likely used because cats always seem to escape death incidents that occurred during that time. Cats are inbred with unbelievable ways of twisting and balancing themselves to help save them in those close death experiences. Adding their unique ability to move quickly, this enables them to miss being hit and killed by moving vehicles. In modern times, cats have survived and landed on their feet after falling from several stories of a building. So, you can easily see why people might say or think cats have nine lives.

It seems that for many people cats just seem to appear out of nowhere and we take them into homes to live. During that stay, when cats are kept inside eventually, they outsmarted the owner and get outside in spite of all efforts for the owner to keep them inside. They may stay away for one day or as many days as they decide to be gone. Usually when they get hungry after trying to kill something to eat outside with no success, they will suddenly just appear one day back out of nowhere just like they did when someone took them in to care for. Water does not seem to be an issue when a cat goes missing for days. For whatever reason, cats don't seem to need much water to survive as humans or other animals do. They find ways to get water one way or another being very observant in looking for water sources. In some instances when cats disappear, they never return. Riley has some comments to make about what can happen to cats when they disappear.

*First of all, to set the record straight from the cat's mouth (so to speak), contrary to what has been said and what some people are sure that they know about cats having nine lives, we don't. Plain and simple, no other explanation needed, WE DON'T HAVE NINE LIVES!! We have one life on earth and only God knows for sure if that will continue afterward or not. Most cat lovers (and dog lovers, for that matter) certainly do hope that we will be reunited after both have passed away. Thinking of heavenly things, if that does happen, wouldn't it be fantastic if we could universally talk and understand each other. WOW!! Wouldn't that be cool or what?? If that were to happen sometime, that sure makes it something to look forward to on the heavenly side.

Anyway, back to the subject at hand, surviving outside of a protected home. We like to sleep, rest in the daytime and exploring in the light or dark. It's our nature. I can tell you for sure of some really close and scary moments when I was in the wild outside of my protected environment. I will go more into detail about those adventures later in the story. For right now, I'll give you just what happens sometimes when I get outside. First, I immediately put into my thoughts and actions of going or being on the defense for safety and living longer reasons. You won't believe just how hard those bird's beaks are when they dive for my head. I've had it happen dozens of times, but one time I moved just right and in time to catch a mockingbird or scissor tail doing it. That was a very rewarding dinner later that day. I have to look out for some humans and all dogs. It's a fact many humans cannot stand us at all. It's also a fact that if dogs see us, it's their nature to bark and try to catch us. What's really funny is for most dogs, if/when they catch us, they don't know what to do when we growl, show our teeth, and sharp paws all at once. One good swipe of a foot full of five sharp claws across that sensitive nose is about all it takes for them to whimper off and leave us alone.

Talk about a cat survival experience, here's a true story of why people might think cats have nine lives. The date of this television report was on March 30, 2017. Our ABC television affiliated WFAA-Channel 8 reported a golden/orange tabby was spotted in Dallas by a homeowner. The report did not say if the cat was male or female. The "new" owner of this cat decided to take it to a veterinarian to see if an identification chip had been implanted in the cat. There was one. It gave the person's name and other identifying information on the chip scan reader. They called the number, and a person answered the call. That call ended up being to Denver, CO. The person stated that the cat went missing from their home sometime in the middle of July 2016. Now, eight months later it shows up in Dallas, TX. Of course, someone might have taken the cat while staying in Denver at that time. I choose not to believe that story. Knowing what I've learned about cats while writing this book, I believe that cat walked, ran, hide, killed for food, found water to drink for each and every step it took from Denver to Dallas. That distance is about 789 miles. If this cat could talk, I'm sure there would be stories "that'd curl your hair"!!

Did Curiosity Kill the Cat?

Somewhere along the way in time, this question started being passed around about cats. It was started when cats got into some very dangerous situations while "exploring" the environment where they were at the time. Hearing that cats might possess living nine lives, they concluded, "Then, just how does a cat finally die?" By or through being curious and not seemly being able to get out of a very dangerous, unsafe situation alive becomes the answer.

I am sure that because of their curiosity many cats have been killed over time. So, the answer to this question would be a definite yes. Health issues with cats can cause death at any age. One dysfunction that occurs with cats is called chronic renal syndrome. According to our veterinarian, Dr. Charles Blonien over half the cats he seen over his years of practice die of C. R. S. This will be discussed with specific details later in a chapter.

*Hey, we got to die someway. If saying this about us answers their question, let it be so. I can attest that I have found myself being curious about something and almost not making it out alive. I do remember a few times when I allowed myself to focus on only what I intended to do turned into something that I was not expecting to happen. Several times this involved seeing something move across a street. I studied it more closely then I darted out into the street without noticing a car was coming along the way minding their own business. They did not see me or what I was doing and, whew, that could have been it for me.

Can You Teach a Cat New Tricks?

Yes, cats can be taught new tricks such as fetching. Remember, this will only happen if THEY want to do it. It takes patience and using little tricks on them to make this work. In other words, one must use their imagination and creativity to make it work. If, after trying to use the creative ways are tried, they don't respond and just sit looking at you, move on and forget it. The best time to make this work is when they are young and in a more playful mood. People have shared and shown me that this is possible. Dogs seem to be able to do and learn to fetch at just about any age. With cats, one must take an entirely different approach for this to work. Once a cat evaluates the situation entirely of what they need to do, it is still totally up to them to decide if they want to do it or not.

*Anytime anyone tries to make me do something that I've decided I don't want to do, there's no way that I will do it until I decide if I want to do it. Sorry, but that's just the way it is and how I think.

A smart cat owner will discover this to be true and will have to accept that is just the way it is with no if's, and's, or but's about it. It's just in the cat's personality and how they operate their thinking process when it comes to most all things in their life.

Don't expect cats to do "tricks" like dogs or other animals do. Has anyone ever seen a cat sit up, roll over, shake hands, or play dead? Apparently, being ask or convinced to do what a dog does really doesn't appeal to them at all. They are not impressed and do not need to participate in such activities.

Playing with my tail in a teasing way may not be considered a trick, but it sure seems fun and tricky for me at the same time. At first, I may show that I don't want anyone to touch my tail. My tail is one of the most sensitive parts of my body. I use it constantly when I'm balancing or walking along the top of a fence or a roofline. When a person starts gently stroking my tail, I like it. After a while I don't mind them grabbing my tail and putting a gentle grip to hold it there for a moment. When I put a waving motion for them to let go and they still gently hold it just enough not to let it go, I really like that to happen. Then, when I do the same again just a little more forceful and they let go of my tail, I love doing that over and over until one of us gets tired of doing it.

What Cats Enjoy Most

It seems that they really like to be given attention the most. They want to be pleased and in doing so they feel this pleases the person back in return. Once a cat has established trust in the person, they become friendlier toward that person. Let's discuss how to attain trust with a cat or most any other animal for that matter.

Trust is the foundation that builds or destroys all human relationships. It is the same with animals. Cats will start out automatically trusting a person from just a simple, gentle touch of petting them on their head or back. It appears that from this action alone, they instinctively and immediately determine if they are going to like that person or not. They love gentle, soft touches at first. Later, they will show you if they want more aggressive and harder petting. This is shown when they use their head to push very hard against your hand. They are giving permission for you to be more aggressive when petting them. They will move away from you if they are not ready for a more aggressive action. Eventually, they will come back to give you another try to please them.

*Oh, boy. There's nothing finer than a person knowing just how to touch me. I love being scratched on my ears especially at the base where they attach to my head. Soft, gentle strokes feel so good. Sometimes, I like the scratching to be harder. When I do, I'll push my head harder toward the hand. After the ears, I love soft touches on my chin. At first, I may not let anyone touch my feet, but after I get to know the person, I like soft touches on my front legs to my toes. One of the most sensitive places on my body is my mid-back to the base of my tail. That area rarely gets touched much less scratched. I can stand hard or soft touches there. Sometimes, even harder the better works for me. When I get enough of the scratching, I'll just

move to get away from it. When I do, do not take it personally. That's just me telling you that I've had enough for the time being.

When a cat is totally enjoying the experience, they may start "purring". Purring is a sound from their vocal cords in the throat. Almost always when a cat purrs, they are letting people know that they are happy or content. A cat's purring can be compared to a dog's wagging tail or a person's smile. Sometimes before they get set in the place they enjoy most (i.e., on a person's lap or stomach), they will take their front paws and push down with alternating paw movement. When this occurs, it's called "kneading". When a cat kneads, they are communicating several messages. It is a natural motion that most cats will do from time to time. Researchers believe this motion is instinctive and is used to stimulate milk from the mother when they nurse as kittens. This becomes a form of communication they remember to be very pleasing to them and should be taken as such when kneading takes place somewhere on the person.

When a cat "squints" their eyes during a scratching episode, this tells the person that their scratching has reached the most ultimate pleasure for the cat.

*One action that I really enjoy doing is licking the condensation off the side of a glass. Not all my relatives will do this. Maybe they just haven't discovered it yet. This is one reason I usually check what my owner is drinking every time I'm close to him. I enjoy it so much if I'm not doing anything else like sleeping or just not paying attention, I will go immediately to see if there is water on the outside of what my owner's drink. For whatever reason, getting licks from the side of a cold drink tastes so good to me. I want to lick that glass until every bit of it has been licked. I discovered slowly dripping water from the bathroom faucet one time and started

licking it. For some unknown reason that water tasted so good to me. Now, I rarely go past that faucet without checking it for a quick drink.

Researchers really don't have a good explanation why condensation on a drink appeals to a cat's fancy. Some say that after a cat sees the condensation and lick it once, they are hooked thereafter. My three reasons are given. One, condensed water has no chemicals in it, and it taste better to the cat. Two, the cooler temperature of the glass feels different on their tongue. Three, it's just another one of those quirky things that cats do on their own.

What Cats Don't Like

Cats are very independent. It seems they can do just about anything that they want. It's only people or other animals getting in the way sometimes to try and stop them. They don't like it when that happens. Cats apparently don't mind challenges put in their path. They don't like it when a person or animals outsmart them. However, if they are not caught or killed, they rethink how to conquer that challenge the next time it happens. Experience in this case, really does pay off for them. Cats don't like being retained when they get into a situation that feels uncomfortable, unusual, or "doesn't feel right" to them. When this happens, just let them go. Trying to stop them only causes more problems. A cat's backup systems for protection (scratching, biting, or whatever works) will engage to that person's dismay.

They don't like loud noises. When they hear anything louder than normal for them, they will immediately react by running away from it. They don't like quick moving motions that are not common to them. Instinctively, they know when something does not feel right and will retreat immediately to get away quickly as far as possible for their own safety, protection, or survival.

*Call me cat crazy or whatever. It's been said that cats are skittish. If you were in our skin, you'd understand why. We are wired in the brain to react as we do when different situations confront us. Just stop and think about being a cat for a moment. You will quickly see why we appear to be skittish. Thank goodness, we were given the ability to move quicker than most all other animals around us including humans.

Cats are said to be finicky.

*Hey, we don't like to be called finicky. Most of us prefer meticulous instead. That sounds more sophisticated. I will admit that there have been times that

I might have been a little picky, not finicky. Being finicky implies that we are vain and to indecisive. We just have certain ways of doing things that sometimes we don't even understand why.

Cats do not like anyone stepping on their tail. Usually, this is by accident when a person does not see the cat especially if it's a dark or black cat in a dark place. That "scream" is a message of immediate pain. At that point, the cat only wants to get away and usually hides someplace. When he feels safe, he will return to normal behavior.

Cats do not like to be declawed on all four of their paws. Only the front paws should be taken when declawing takes place. Taking all four claws away from them can be a death sentence for them. Cats need their back claws for climbing purposes when needed. They also need their back claws for defensive reasons when they find themselves in a position to fight off other animals and any person who is trying to do harm to them. Cats with no claws seem to develop neurotic behaviors. This could be compared to telling a human boxer to go into the ring without their boxing gloves on. The much bigger gloves would have a definite advantage over the opponent without them. I've had cat owners tell me that they made a big mistake taking away all their cat's claws.

People listen to me. When you take away my back claws, it leaves me defenseless when trying to defend myself when I get into those situations. Besides this does not allow me to scratch myself anywhere on my body when I itch of when I need them to clean myself better. When I get dirty and I can't clean an area with my paws, it drives me crazy.

How Do Cats Talk? What Does That Meow Mean?

Anyone who has owned a cat will learn that cat's meow in different ways. When a cat is hungry, they will loudly meow to get your attention. When they see that they have the person's attention, they will go over to their food bowl and meow even louder if someone is not following him to the bowl. I've observed that when a cat is being followed, he will quickly check to see if someone is following him. When he does this, you cannot see their eyes. Apparently, their peripheral vision is wider than humans. When they are outside, cats can "throw" their meow's long distance. This is accomplished by "yelling" in a higher pitched voice. Once I was walking our dog Tanna (our Airedale) and our cat was already outside and saw us. He was at least 300 ft. away and he let out a meow that sound like he was right beside us. I couldn't believe it! I'm sure they use this voice when they are lost or need help anytime.

Yes, we can do all kinds of amazing things when the situation requires such action. Sometimes we even amaze ourselves at all we can do. I think I remember that day.

I saw you and Tanna way off from me. Part of that loud meow being so loud was that I'd just gotten into a cat fight with that big old cat. We called him Tubbie who lives down the street from us. Part of that loud meow was that I had just come out of the battle alive with a few bites and scratches but was really ticked off at that cat!!

When a cat knows that something is about to happen, they will let out a quiet low-pitched meow several times in just a few seconds. That's to let the person know they are willing to do what is expected of them in that situation. Guess one could say that the cat is trying to meow its way out of doing something he really doesn't want to do.

Another way cats talk is with their ears, believe it or not. Communication is done with and through a cat's ears. When knowing what you are looking for, ear movements can provide a lot of information regarding a cat's mood or next course of action. For example, cats that are content and happy tend to have eyes that are wide open or maybe a little closed. Cat owners can read a cat's mood in additional forms of body language, such as by the simple way they hold their ears. There are at least four different ways that cats express their feelings through their ears, from emotions like curiosity and uneasiness to agitation and fear. These four emotions include: **Curious**-the ears will move in an upward direction. Owners may notice that even during cat naps, the ears will move towards even the most subtle noises. **Uneasy**-If a cat feels threatened or uneasy, ears turn toward the side. They look a bit like airplane wings jutting from each side off the head. Sideway facing ears are also more protected. Consider airplane ears to be an early warning sign to back off and stop whatever has taken place to make the cat feel threatened. **Agitated**-flickering ears may indicate rising agitation. The sideways-facing ears flutter or vibrate very quickly, in reaction to high arousal. If this persists it could also be a sign of a health problem. If the agitation continues causing the arousal does not go away, the cat may progress to threat and may attack. **Angry or Scared**-fearful or angry cats flatten their ears tightly to the head or position them backward. This keeps the ears out of range of claws or teeth, in preparation for either fight or flight. Cats with slicked back ears may attack if their assailant ignores the warning. Ears can become a warning sign as to what the cat may do next and helps owners anticipate and avoid potential problems.

A quick, loud meow usually indicates someone has stepped on the cat's tail.

Ouch!! That really does hurt. We have very sensitive nerve endings all the way to the tip of our tails. That's why we sometimes like people to play gently with our tails. Don't expect us to allow you to touch our tails until we have learned to trust you. Once that is established, let's play games with my tail. When I move away, it simply means that I've had enough. Don't take it personal.

When I'm petting Riley sometimes, it seems to help me open my mind and different, creative thoughts seem to cross my thinking. There have been several times that I have felt sympathy for animals, especially for those who have been mistreated. Abusing animals is the same as abusing humans. The abuse is imprinted in their brain. Their memories of the abuse stay with them forever. When those old memories come back to them, they proceed with caution of whatever that fear might be an example would be like feeding them. They will give you a look with sad eyes anticipating what's going to happen next. Staying away from the food until you leave is a strong indicator that someone abused them using food as a way to abuse them. They show their appreciation back to us in several ways. Some are more obvious than others. What really gets to my heart is they have this feeling that they can't describe to us. How frustrating that must be. How would it be if humans did not have a way to express one of the strongest human emotions this world has to offer? How could we express or explain why we do as humans when experiencing very emotional experiences in our lives? When viewed in this sense, love takes on a new and more powerful emotion in our lives. It saddens my heart when dogs and cats experience love from us but cannot give it a name. What helps me to understand this better is to realize that even though animals cannot verbally express it, they know exactly what it is through our actions and yes, even telling them that they are loved. Maybe, just maybe, I'd like to think they will know what love really means by the way we touch them or other actions that are loving and endearing to them.

"Dogs have two missions in living: barking and smelling other dog's rear ends.

Cats have two missions too: to be curious like a cat checking out any little detail and to prowl around the neighbor."

author's original quote

as of 11-26-21

People think that cats are difficult to understand. Try being a cat and thinking about understanding humans.

Purring….What's That All About?

Purring is a sound from the cat's vocal cords that usually indicates happiness or contentment. Cats purring is the same as a dog wagging its tail or a human smiling. A cat's purr begins in the brain. A repetitive neural oscillator signal is sent to the throat muscles causing them to twitch 50 to 100 vibrations per second. This causes the vocal cords to separate when the cat inhales and exhales creating a purr. It can occur when a cat is injured or in pain. Research has shown when a cat purrs many signals are sent to their brain. Those signals relax an injured cat and healing starts to take place immediately when this happens.

Contrary to popular belief, cats are not the only animals that purr. Purring or purring like sounds are also made by raccoons, rabbits, squirrels, guinea pigs, and badgers.

When I purr, I'm letting you know that whatever you're doing to me, I like it. Purring calms me down. When I purr, I am in total peace of mind.

Experienced cat owners over time also develop a sense of peace and calmness within themselves when they hear their cat purr. Giving the cat pleasure seems to work the same for the person causing the purr to occur, so to speak. Put another way, "*When a purr occurs, peace and tranquility endures.*" (original quote by author, 3-31-18)

Thinking Processes of the Cat: Feelings, Emotions, or Jerk Reactions

I'd like to start with explaining what jerk reactions mean. Sometimes after Riley has been detained in the house for an extended amount of time, all of a sudden, I will hear some thrashing around action away from me. Usually, I can't see him or what he is doing. Suddenly, he will jump upon the bed or wherever and go into what I'd call "a cat panic attack". His ears will be pinned back somewhat, he will have this unusual look in his eyes, and his actions will be quick and jerky. It's like he has this burst of energy that takes him over.

Sometimes, out of nowhere, I get these overwhelming feelings that I can't control. It seems like I need to just move around quickly like I'm in a battle to survive. My male owner seems to have learned how to help me calm down after a while. Sometimes, after I do this, he then let's me go outside. I never know when I'm going to do this. It seems to start in my mind and just kind of takes me over. When I'm finished, I don't feel any different. Letting out that burst of energy feels good to me.

Cats and Cleanliness

Cats use their forepaws for saliva to act as a washcloth for their face and other areas of their bodies. This is why they lick themselves all the time, but especially after finished eating. Cats rarely need baths. First, they freak out by the sound of a running faucet if it's too close to them. More than likely, the very first experience of getting bathed was not a pleasant event at all. Those memories come back quickly, and they don't want to have anything to do with that again. Second, they clean themselves naturally, instinctively. For the most part, cats do not need to be bathed unless they have a total mess over their body or small areas that need to be cleaned especially on their back.

We like to feel clean all the time. Therefore, we lick ourselves over and over until we feel refreshed. For those of us who shed hair more than others, this action may cause us to lick too much hair and we swallow it. Our stomachs do not like this, and we will regurgitate (an impressive word to show you just how smart I really am). Sorry about that mess this makes. This is better than all that hair getting passed through my stomach. When that happens, it really messes with my entire digestive system. If we don't pass that in a litter box and then stop eating, it's time to visit that wonderful place called the veterinarian's office. More about this adventure follows.

A Trip to the Veterinarians Clinic

I know they will make me feel better, but I sure don't like getting out where so many other animals are found in one place and the same time. It's just too much for me to process at one time, especially when I'm locked into a cage where I can't get out and away from all that mess. And the smells in there with all those animals are at once plus the others who had been in earlier does not agree with my stomach really well. Once I get in to see the vet., I'm getting calmed down if something loud like a dog barking or a dog fight breaks out has taken place. Usually, the vets are very gentle, and I like them.

How I Taught People to Open Doors for Me

It's amazing how cats learn to get their way. One way is to start meowing lowly and soft. If no one makes a move to the door, a second meow is given only it's a little louder with a hint of "I need to go outside, and no one is listening to me." Many times, the cat will be at either the front or back door already….waiting for someone to help him. If no one still doesn't respond, here comes the third meow warning. This third meow is louder and longer than the other two. If no one comes, he'll just start walking around usually trying to find a comfortable place to wait it out.

Yes, humans just don't get it. They should be at a moment's notice of giving me all their attention and giving ME what I want. I learned over time that it just takes a lot of persistence plus a humongous, annoying meow to get them to move for me. When I want some food or water, all I have to do is go over to my food bowl and do a gentle meow. If they don't come after a while, I'll wait and give them some time to get my food. After that, I just stand by my empty food bowl do several a little meows one right after another until someone hears me and fills the bowl. I usually want outside to get some exercise and fresh air. There's a litter box in the room across from the food and waters bowls. I use that cat litter box about half the time inside and half the time outside.

Put Me in a Cat Carry Cage, NO WAY!

I knew something was wrong, but I didn't quite know what it was. I hadn't been feeling myself lately. I didn't quite know how to describe it with the limited English, I knew. There's just something that doesn't jive with me when anyone tries to force me into doing something that I do not feel comfortable in doing. And so, it is with trying to catch me and then trying to put me into one of those mobile cat carrying containers. I will put up a big struggle with one person, but when they team up on me with two people, it's just too much for me to overcome.

Salvation- The Cross on Riley's Back

This short little chapter will be a little personal for many. A person's spiritual condition should be spoken of freely and sometimes more openly than we do. Satan is always trying to pull us away from God. That is why non-believers should repeat the sinner's prayer and then put those words into action. People are different. Some may rejoice that they have been forgiven to start all over again with God. Others may say is that it and reflect on the true meaning of what just happened at a later date. **Christ's crucifixion represents Jesus dying on a cross to take away our sins.** Yes, Christians will continue to sin in different ways. As long as each of us are alive here, we will be tempted to sin. God knows and understands that, but He is always listening for the person to ask for forgiveness so that they continue with a sin free life as much as they possibly can. Forgiveness is a powerful word of action that everyone should take forgiveness to heart with its good intentions. If you have not accepted Christ as your Savior, the time is now to do so. From what is said in the Bible about Christ returning to earth for those who believe by their faith, the timing could not be any better than now. Stop fighting it!! Accept Jesus now so that you may live a heavenly eternal life. Do not allow Satan to take away your joy in this life. AMEN.

Closing Thoughts

These are some conclusions that I have learned about cats since I started writing about Riley.

"Practically any person can get a cat to do anything, but only if the cat first decides that it wants to do it or not."

"You can lead a cat to water, but there's no way it will drink unless IT decides to do so. The more force one uses, the more aggressive the cat will become to get totally away from the situation. **Caution here: Watch out for scratching claws or teeth bites that WILL bleed if one continues to force the issue.**"

"Cats control us because we can't control them, and they know it."

"Usually, a person who feels that they must control their lives and others around them, will hate cats. Why? Because they learn very quickly that the cat will not allow anyone to control them….never, ever."

"Raising a family is at times much like trying to herd cats."

"Cats give a whole new meaning to gentleness and how to utilize it in our lives."

"Over time my cat taught me the importance of patience and the power of a gentle touch."

These are some different thoughts and perspectives that have been stated about cats from several people over time. These are my favorite twenty of the many that I have read. It's amazing how many people have made comments about cats over many years. The following quotes are from some very interesting people. Read them, study them, look for deeper meanings, look for humorous thoughts, enjoy them and laugh.

"Time spent with cats is never wasted." Sigmund Freud (psychotherapist)

"As every cat owner knows, nobody really owns a cat." Ellen Perry Berkeley

"In ancient times cats were worshipped as gods; they have not forgotten this." Terry Pratchett

"A cat is a puzzle for which there is no solution." Hazel Nicholson

"Dogs eat. Cats dine." Ann Taylor

"Cats are connoisseurs of comfort." James Herriot (author, All Creatures Great and Small)

"Meow means 'woof' in a cat." George Carlin (comedian)

"A meow massages the heart." Stuart McMillan

"All cats like being the focus of attention." Peter Gray

"The phrase 'domestic cat' is an oxymoron." George Will (columnist, television correspondent)

"Authors like cats because they are such quiet, lovable, wise creatures, and cats like authors for the same reasons." Robertson Davies

"If you are worthy of its affection, a cat will be your friend, but never your slave." Theophile Gautier

"The mathematical probability of a common cat doing exactly as it pleases is the one scientific absolute in this world." Lynn M. Osband

"The key to a successful new relationship between a cat and human is patience (and gentleness, added by the author)." Susan Easterly

"A cat will do what it wants when it wants, and there's not a thing you can do about it." Frank Perkins

"Cats choose us; we don't own them." Kristin Cast (author, House of Night series)

"Cats have it all....admiration, an endless sleep, and company only when they want it." Rod McKuen (poet, Stanyan Street & Other Sorrows)

"There are two means of refuge from the miseries of life: music and cats." Albert Schweitzer (physician, theologian, musician, philosopher)

"Of all God's creatures, there is only one that cannot be made slave of the lash/leash. That one is the cat. If man could be crossed with the cat it would improve the man, but it would deteriorate the cat." Mark Twain (author, The Adventures of Tom Sawyer)

"If a dog jumps into your lap, it is because he is fond of you. If a cat does the same thing it is because your lap is warmer." A. N. Whitehead (mathematician and philosopher)

"Time spent with cats is never wasted." Sigmund Freud (psychotherapist)

"As every cat owner knows, nobody really owns a cat." Ellen Perry Berkeley

"In ancient times cats were worshipped as gods; they have not forgotten this." Terry Pratchett

"A cat is a puzzle for which there is no solution." Hazel Nicholson

"Dogs eat. Cats dine." Ann Taylor

"Cats are connoisseurs of comfort." James Herriot (author, <u>All Creatures Great and Small</u>)

"Meow means 'woof' in a cat." George Carlin (comedian)

"A meow massages the heart." Stuart McMillan

"All cats like being the focus of attention." Peter Gray

"The phrase 'domestic cat' is an oxymoron." George Will (columnist, television correspondent)

"Authors like cats because they are such quiet, lovable, wise creatures, and cats like authors for the same reasons." Robertson Davies

"If you are worthy of its affection, a cat will be your friend, but never your slave." Theophile Gautier

"The mathematical probability of a common cat doing exactly as it pleases is the one scientific absolute in this world." Lynn M. Osband

"The key to a successful new relationship between a cat and human is patience (and gentleness, added by the author)." Susan Easterly

"A cat will do what it wants when it wants, and there's not a thing you can do about it." Frank Perkins

"Cats choose us; we don't own them." Kristin Cast (author, House of Night series)

"Cats have it all....admiration, an endless sleep, and company only when they want it." Rod McKuen (poet, Stanyan Street & Other Sorrows)

"There are two means of refuge from the miseries of life: music and cats." Albert Schweitzer (physician, theologian, musician, philosopher)

"Of all God's creatures, there is only one that cannot be made slave of the lash/leash. That one is the cat. If man could be crossed with the cat it would improve the man, but it would deteriorate the cat." Mark Twain (author, The Adventures of Tom Sawyer)

"If a dog jumps into your lap, it is because he is fond of you. If a cat does the same thing it is because your lap is warmer." A. N. Whitehead (mathematician and philosopher)

FINAL THOUGHTS

Dogs are so loyal. They look forward to seeing us each and every day. They never forget all the good things we do for them.

Whereas cats on the other hand only care about eating and getting back outside to "cruise" their area properties for any changes that have been made by humans and to look for other cats. This practice has become known as: Tom Catting Around.

POSTNOTE: I'M STILL A DOG LOVER FIRST. HOWEVER, AFTER THE EXPERIENCES THAT I HAVE HAD WITH THIS CAT OVER NUMEROUS YEARS, I MUST SAY THAT I HAVE ATTAINED A WHOLE NEW PERSPECTIVE ABOUT CATS.

I hope that you have enjoyed reading this book. I have tried to give practical information, some educational material about cats, and some humor along with the reading. Thank you for reading it and especially for buying it to read to children.

On a sad note, Mr. Kitty died of C. R. S. on Tuesday, January 14, 2020, at 12:04 pm. I have missed him dearly and hope to see him again someday where we could really talk to one another.

Bob A. Jackson, M.S.

Plano, TX.

1-14-22